Tennessee
The Volunteer State

Tika Downey

PowerKiDS press™

New York

Published in 2010 by The Rosen Publishing Group, Inc.
29 East 21st Street, New York, NY 10010

First Edition

Editor: Joanne Randolph
Book Layout: Kate Laczynski
Book Design: Greg Tucker
Photo Researcher: Jessica Gerweck

Photo Credits: Cover © Richard Cummins/Corbis; pp. 5, 11, 15, 22 (tree, animal, bird, flower) Shutterstock.com; pp. 7, 22 (Sequoyah) MPI/Getty Images; pp. 9, 19 Gavin Hellier/Getty Images; p. 13 Harrison Shull/Getty Images; p. 13 (inset) Gail Shumway/Getty Images; p. 17 © Walter Bibikow/ age fotostock; p. 22 (Davy Crockett) Hulton Archive/Getty Images; p. 22 (Miley Cyrus) Lester Cohen/ WireImage/Getty Images.

Library of Congress Cataloging-in-Publication Data

Downey, Tika.
   Tennessee : the Volunteer State / Tika Downey. — 1st ed.
      p. cm. — (Our amazing states)
   Includes index.
   ISBN 978-1-4358-9352-8 (library binding) — ISBN 978-1-4358-9800-4 (pbk.) —
ISBN 978-1-4358-9801-1 (6-pack)
   1. Tennessee—Juvenile literature. I. Title.
   F436.3.D69 2010
   976.8—dc22
                                        2009023030

Manufactured in the United States of America

CPSIA Compliance Information: Batch #WW10PK: For Further Information contact Rosen Publishing, New York, New York at 1-800-237-9932

Contents

The Volunteer State   4

Tennessee in Times Past   6

What Does the Land Look Like?   8

Take a Walk on the Wild Side   10

Business Keeps Getting Better   12

Nashville Is Neat   14

The Hermitage   16

Mighty Memphis   18

Visiting the Volunteer State   20

Glossary   21

Tennessee at a Glance   22

Index   24

Web Sites   24

The Volunteer State

What do you know about Tennessee? It is famous for its early **pioneers** and for the three U.S. presidents who lived there, Andrew Jackson, James Polk, and Andrew Johnson. It is famous today for things as different as country music, new forms of **energy**, and cars built by robots! Tennessee is often called the **Volunteer** State because Tennessee's people are quick to volunteer to help their country in times of war.

Tennessee is in the eastern United States. North Carolina is east of it. Virginia and Kentucky are north of it. The Mississippi River and Arkansas form the western border. Mississippi, Alabama, and Georgia are south of Tennessee.

The Great Smoky Mountains, shown here, run between Tennessee and North Carolina. The Great Smokies are some of the oldest mountains in the world.

Tennessee in Times Past

Native Americans, such as the Cherokee and Chickasaw, have lived in Tennessee for about 8,000 years. Spanish **explorer** Hernando de Soto arrived in 1540. Around 1700, French explorers built **forts** near Memphis and Nashville. England took over the area in 1763. In 1783, the United States won its freedom from England. Tennessee became the sixteenth state in 1796.

During the **Civil War**, Tennessee and other Southern states fought to become their own country, the Confederate States of America. Many battles, such as the Battle of Shiloh, were fought in Tennessee. After the North won the war in 1865, Tennessee quickly rejoined the United States.

The Battle of Shiloh was fought in Tennessee on April 6 and 7, 1862. The Union won the battle, but there were heavy losses on both sides.

What Does the Land Look Like?

Tennessee land looks different based on where you are. The Blue **Ridge**, in the east, includes the Great Smoky Mountains and Clingmans Dome. Clingmans Dome is Tennessee's tallest mountain at 6,643 feet (2,025 m). The Gulf Coastal Plain is part of a huge plain that begins at the Gulf of Mexico! In between the mountains and this plain are the Appalachian Valley and Ridge **Province**, the Cumberland **Plateau**, the Highland Rim, and the Nashville **Basin**. The three largest rivers are the Mississippi, the Tennessee, and the Cumberland.

Summers are warm and winters are cool in Tennessee. Tennessee is also very wet. It gets about 52 inches (132 cm) of **precipitation** yearly!

This is Ruby Falls, which is deep inside Lookout Mountain. The waterfall is 145 feet (44 m) tall.

Take a Walk on the Wild Side

What do you picture when you imagine Tennessee? If you said "forests," then you are right. Forests cover half the state. There are more than 200 kinds of trees in Tennessee, including **poplar**, maple, oak, elm, pine, walnut, and cherry.

Many animals live throughout the state. You can find deer, bears, beavers, opossums, otters, and even wild hogs. There are also turkeys, songbirds, frogs, and 32 kinds of snakes.

One common animal is the state's official wild animal, the raccoon. Its black mask and bushy, ringed tail make it easy to recognize. Raccoons often live in hollow trees or the ground and come out at night.

This baby raccoon stands on a log in the forest. Raccoons eat almost anything, including berries, seeds, frogs, bird eggs, and even pet food!

Business Keeps Getting Better

Tennessee has factories that make all sorts of goods. Did you know that many cars and trucks are made in Tennessee? Boats and airplane parts are as well. There are factories that make computers, machines, and metal goods, too. Some factories make food. If you had bread, cereal, or candy today, it might have come from Tennessee.

Tennessee's farms produce beef, chicken, pigs, eggs, and milk. They grow crops such as cotton, corn, tobacco, soybeans, and hay, too. Some farmers also raise a famous kind of horse called the Tennessee walking horse. Another way Tennessee makes money is by selling electricity. It produces enough electricity for an area about twice the size of the state.

Here you can see the rich farmlands near Jasper, Tennessee. *Inset:* The Tennessee walking horse is know for its smooth gait, or the way it walks and runs.

Nashville Is Neat

You may have heard of Nashville. It is world famous as Music City, USA, the center of country music. It has many places to record music. You can visit the Country Music Hall of Fame and **Museum** or see country music shows at the Grand Ole Opry.

Nashville is also Tennessee's capital. A famous builder named William Strickland planned the state capitol. Strickland and President James Polk are both buried there.

What else can you do in Nashville? You can learn about the state's history at the Tennessee State Museum. You can visit the Adventure Science Center or, just outside the city center, you can see Belle Meade **Plantation**, which was built in 1853.

Here you can see many of the buildings in downtown Nashville. The Tennessee State House is the building at the bottom of this photo with the bluish roof.

The Hermitage

If you are interested in history, the Hermitage is a great place to visit. The Hermitage is near Nashville and was President Andrew Jackson's home for about 40 years. Jackson bought the Hermitage in 1804, when it was a farm with a log farmhouse. He bought more land to create a huge plantation. He raised cotton to sell and other crops to supply food for his family and slaves. He also raised racehorses.

Around 1820, Jackson had a large brick home built for his family and a fancy garden made for his wife. Jackson died at the Hermitage in 1845. Today, you can visit the Hermitage. It is like a living history book!

"Hermitage" means "a quiet country place." If you go to the Hermitage, you can see the house, garden, slave cabins, a church, and the place where Jackson and his wife are buried.

Mighty Memphis

Although Nashville is the capital, Memphis is Tennessee's largest city. It is an important business center, and many goods pass through the city on their way to other places.

Like Nashville, Memphis is famous for music. It is known for blues music, which talks about life's hardships, and for rock music. Memphis was home to W. C. Handy, a well-known blues songwriter, and to Elvis Presley, one of the most famous rock singers ever. Today, you can go to Handy's home and Presley's home, which is called Graceland. You can also visit the Stax Museum of American Soul Music. The city has many art and history museums. You can also visit a very old Native American village called Chucalissa.

In 1950, Sun Studios opened on Beale Street in Memphis. Rock-and-roll greats, such as Elvis Presley and Johnny Cash, recorded music there.

Visiting the Volunteer State

Millions of people visit Tennessee every year because there are so many things to do. Many go to Nashville and Memphis for the music, or they visit singer Dolly Parton's Dollywood theme park to see live music shows and have fun.

Some people like to visit the art museums. Others like to go to history museums and places like James Polk's home, Civil War battlefields, and the Casey Jones Home and Railroad Museum. Some enjoy the American Museum of Science and Energy in Oak Ridge. Tennessee has many famous zoos and aquariums, too. People who enjoy hiking and camping may visit the mountains or state parks. What would you like to do in Tennessee?

Glossary

basin (BAY-sin) An area of low land.

energy (EH-nur-jee) The power to work or to act.

explorer (ek-SPLOR-ur) Someone who travels and looks for new land.

forts (FORTS) Strong buildings or places that can be guarded against enemies.

museum (myoo-ZEE-um) A place where art or historical pieces are safely kept for people to see and to study.

pioneers (py-uh-NEERZ) The first people to settle in a new area.

plantation (plan-TAY-shun) A very large farm where crops are grown.

plateau (pla-TOH) A broad, flat, high piece of land.

poplar (PAH-pler) A tall tree that grows quickly and has wide leaves.

precipitation (preh-sih-pih-TAY-shun) Any moisture that falls from the sky. Rain and snow are precipitation.

province (PRAH-vins) A part of a country.

ridge (RIJ) A long, narrow chain of hills or mountains.

volunteer (vah-lun-TEER) A person who offers himself for service in the military of his own free will.

Tennessee State Symbols

State Tree
Tulip Poplar

State Animal
Raccoon

State Flag

State Bird
Mockingbird

State Flower
Purple Iris

State Seal

Famous People from Tennessee

Sequoyah
(1770s–1843)
Born in Tuskegee, TN
Invented a writing
system for the Cherokee

David "Davy" Crockett
(1786–1836)
Born near Limestone, TN
Pioneer

Miley Cyrus
(1992–)
Born in Nashville, TN
Singer and Actress

Tennessee State Map

Tennessee State Facts

Nickname: The Volunteer State

Population: 6,214,888

Area: 42,143 square miles (109,150 sq km)

Motto: "Agriculture and Commerce"

Index

A
Arkansas, 4

C
Cherokee, 6
Country Music Hall of Fame
  and Museum, 14

E
energy, 4, 20

F
forts, 6

G
Georgia, 4

J
Jackson, Andrew, 4, 16
Johnson, Andrew, 4

K
Kentucky, 4

M
Mississippi, 4
Mississippi River, 4, 8
music, 4, 14, 18, 20

N
Nashville Basin, 8
Native Americans, 6
North Carolina, 4

P
Polk, James, 4, 14
poplar, 10
precipitation, 8

R
robots, 4

S
Soto, Hernando de, 6

V
Virginia, 4

W
war, 4, 6

Web Sites

Due to the changing nature of Internet links, PowerKids Press has developed an online list of Web sites related to the subject of this book. This site is updated regularly. Please use this link to access the list:

www.powerkidslinks.com/amst/tn/